50 Ontario Orchard Recipes

By: Kelly Johnson

Table of Contents

- Apple Butter Spread
- Peach Cobbler with Maple Syrup
- Pear and Walnut Salad
- Ontario Apple Crisp
- Plum and Almond Tart
- Strawberry Rhubarb Pie
- Cherry Clafoutis
- Blueberry Maple Muffins
- Raspberry Peach Jam
- Cranberry Apple Chutney
- Spiced Pear Cider
- Baked Apple with Honey and Cinnamon
- Maple-Glazed Peaches
- Blackberry Oatmeal Bars
- Plum and Ginger Compote
- Strawberry Shortcake
- Roasted Pears with Balsamic Drizzle
- Apple and Cheddar Grilled Cheese
- Raspberry Lemon Loaf
- Ontario Peach Salsa
- Wild Blueberry Pancakes
- Spiced Apple Cake
- Pear and Brie Crostini
- Maple Apple Granola
- Cherry Almond Scones
- Cranberry Orange Bread
- Plum Butter Spread
- Strawberry Basil Sorbet
- Peach and Pecan Salad
- Apple Cinnamon Waffles
- Blueberry Lemon Cheesecake
- Blackberry Chia Jam
- Raspberry Almond Tart
- Apple Fritter Donuts
- Plum and Honey Yogurt Parfait

- Ontario Orchard Fruit Salad
- Baked Peaches with Vanilla Ice Cream
- Maple Cranberry Sauce
- Apple Cider Doughnuts
- Peach and Raspberry Galette
- Blueberry Lavender Syrup
- Pear and Maple Smoothie
- Blackberry Honey Butter
- Spiced Plum Cake
- Roasted Apple and Squash Soup
- Strawberry Rhubarb Compote
- Cranberry and Brie Puff Pastry Bites
- Apple Walnut Bread
- Maple Baked Apples with Oat Topping
- Ontario Orchard Harvest Jam

Homemade Apple Butter Spread

Ingredients

- 6 large apples (Granny Smith, Fuji, or Honeycrisp), peeled, cored, and chopped
- 1 cup apple cider (or water)
- 1/2 cup brown sugar
- 1/2 cup granulated sugar
- 1 tsp cinnamon
- 1/2 tsp nutmeg
- 1/4 tsp cloves
- 1 tsp vanilla extract
- Pinch of salt

Instructions

1. **Cook the Apples** – In a large pot or slow cooker, combine the chopped apples and apple cider. Cover and cook on low heat for 6-8 hours, stirring occasionally, until the apples become very soft.
2. **Blend Smooth** – Use an immersion blender to puree the mixture until smooth. Alternatively, transfer to a blender and blend in batches.
3. **Add Spices and Sweeteners** – Stir in brown sugar, granulated sugar, cinnamon, nutmeg, cloves, vanilla extract, and salt.
4. **Simmer to Thicken** – Continue cooking uncovered on low heat for another 1-2 hours, stirring occasionally, until the mixture thickens to a spreadable consistency.
5. **Cool and Store** – Let the apple butter cool completely before transferring it to jars. Store in the refrigerator for up to two weeks or freeze for longer storage.

Peach Cobbler with Maple Syrup

Ingredients

- 4 cups sliced peaches (fresh or frozen)
- 1/4 cup maple syrup
- 1 tbsp lemon juice
- 1 tsp cinnamon
- 1/4 tsp nutmeg
- 1 cup all-purpose flour
- 1/2 cup granulated sugar
- 1 1/2 tsp baking powder
- 1/2 tsp salt
- 1/2 cup milk
- 1/4 cup unsalted butter, melted

Instructions

1. Preheat oven to 375°F (190°C) and grease a baking dish.
2. Toss peaches with maple syrup, lemon juice, cinnamon, and nutmeg, then spread into the dish.
3. In a bowl, whisk flour, sugar, baking powder, and salt. Add milk and melted butter, stirring to form a batter.
4. Spoon batter over peaches and spread evenly.
5. Bake for 35-40 minutes until golden brown. Let cool slightly before serving.

Pear and Walnut Salad

Ingredients

- 4 cups mixed greens (arugula, spinach, or romaine)
- 2 ripe pears, thinly sliced
- 1/2 cup walnuts, toasted
- 1/4 cup crumbled goat cheese or blue cheese
- 1/4 cup dried cranberries
- 2 tbsp olive oil
- 1 tbsp balsamic vinegar
- 1 tsp honey
- Salt and pepper to taste

Instructions

1. In a large bowl, combine mixed greens, pear slices, walnuts, cheese, and cranberries.
2. In a small bowl, whisk olive oil, balsamic vinegar, honey, salt, and pepper.
3. Drizzle dressing over salad and toss gently. Serve immediately.

Ontario Apple Crisp

Ingredients

- 4 cups Ontario apples, peeled and sliced
- 1/4 cup granulated sugar
- 1 tsp cinnamon
- 1 tbsp lemon juice
- 1/2 cup rolled oats
- 1/2 cup brown sugar
- 1/3 cup all-purpose flour
- 1/4 cup unsalted butter, melted

Instructions

1. Preheat oven to 350°F (175°C) and grease a baking dish.
2. Toss apples with granulated sugar, cinnamon, and lemon juice, then spread in the dish.
3. In a bowl, mix oats, brown sugar, flour, and melted butter to form a crumbly topping.
4. Sprinkle over apples and bake for 35-40 minutes until golden brown. Serve warm.

Plum and Almond Tart

Ingredients

- 1 pre-made tart crust
- 4 ripe plums, thinly sliced
- 1/2 cup almond flour
- 1/4 cup granulated sugar
- 1/4 cup unsalted butter, softened
- 1 egg
- 1/2 tsp almond extract
- 1/4 cup sliced almonds

Instructions

1. Preheat oven to 375°F (190°C). Place tart crust in a tart pan and set aside.
2. In a bowl, beat butter and sugar until creamy, then mix in almond flour, egg, and almond extract.
3. Spread almond mixture over the tart crust and arrange plum slices on top.
4. Sprinkle with sliced almonds and bake for 30-35 minutes until golden.

Strawberry Rhubarb Pie

Ingredients

- 2 1/2 cups strawberries, hulled and sliced
- 2 1/2 cups rhubarb, chopped
- 3/4 cup granulated sugar
- 1/4 cup cornstarch
- 1/2 tsp cinnamon
- 1 tbsp lemon juice
- 1 tbsp butter, diced
- 1 egg (for egg wash)
- 1 double pie crust

Instructions

1. Preheat oven to 375°F (190°C). Roll out pie crust into a 9-inch pie pan.
2. In a bowl, mix strawberries, rhubarb, sugar, cornstarch, cinnamon, and lemon juice. Pour into the crust.
3. Dot filling with butter, then top with the second crust. Seal edges and cut slits for steam.
4. Brush with egg wash and bake for 50-55 minutes until golden. Cool before serving.

Cherry Clafoutis

Ingredients

- 2 cups fresh cherries, pitted
- 3 eggs
- 1/2 cup granulated sugar
- 1 cup whole milk
- 1/2 cup all-purpose flour
- 1 tsp vanilla extract
- 1/4 tsp salt
- Powdered sugar for garnish

Instructions

1. Preheat oven to 375°F (190°C) and grease a baking dish.
2. Arrange cherries evenly in the dish.
3. In a blender, mix eggs, sugar, milk, flour, vanilla, and salt. Pour over cherries.
4. Bake for 35-40 minutes until golden and set. Dust with powdered sugar before serving.

Blueberry Maple Muffins

Ingredients

- 1 1/2 cups all-purpose flour
- 1/2 cup rolled oats
- 1/2 cup maple syrup
- 1/2 cup milk
- 1/4 cup butter, melted
- 1 egg
- 1 tsp vanilla extract
- 1 1/2 tsp baking powder
- 1/2 tsp baking soda
- 1/4 tsp salt
- 1 cup fresh blueberries

Instructions

1. Preheat oven to 375°F (190°C). Line a muffin tin with liners.
2. In a bowl, mix flour, oats, baking powder, baking soda, and salt.
3. In another bowl, whisk maple syrup, milk, butter, egg, and vanilla. Combine with dry ingredients.
4. Fold in blueberries and divide into muffin cups.
5. Bake for 18-22 minutes until golden.

Raspberry Peach Jam

Ingredients

- 2 cups raspberries
- 2 cups peaches, peeled and diced
- 2 cups granulated sugar
- 2 tbsp lemon juice
- 1 packet pectin

Instructions

1. In a large pot, combine raspberries, peaches, sugar, and lemon juice. Bring to a boil.
2. Stir in pectin and continue boiling for 5 minutes, stirring constantly.
3. Remove from heat and ladle into sterilized jars. Seal and let cool.

Cranberry Apple Chutney

Ingredients

- 2 cups cranberries
- 2 apples, peeled and diced
- 1/2 cup brown sugar
- 1/2 cup apple cider vinegar
- 1/2 tsp cinnamon
- 1/4 tsp ginger
- 1/4 tsp salt

Instructions

1. In a saucepan, combine all ingredients and bring to a boil.
2. Reduce heat and simmer for 20-25 minutes, stirring occasionally.
3. Cool before transferring to jars.

Spiced Pear Cider

Ingredients

- 6 ripe pears, chopped
- 4 cups water
- 1/2 cup brown sugar
- 1 cinnamon stick
- 3 cloves
- 1/2 tsp nutmeg

Instructions

1. In a pot, combine pears, water, sugar, and spices. Simmer for 45 minutes.
2. Mash pears and strain liquid through a fine sieve. Serve warm.

Baked Apple with Honey and Cinnamon

Ingredients

- 4 apples, cored
- 1/4 cup honey
- 1 tsp cinnamon
- 1/4 cup chopped nuts (optional)
- 1 tbsp butter

Instructions

1. Preheat oven to 375°F (190°C).
2. Place apples in a baking dish and drizzle with honey.
3. Sprinkle with cinnamon and fill centers with nuts. Top each with a small piece of butter.
4. Bake for 30-35 minutes until soft.

Maple-Glazed Peaches

Ingredients

- 4 ripe peaches, halved and pitted
- 1/4 cup maple syrup
- 2 tbsp butter, melted
- 1/2 tsp cinnamon

Instructions

1. Preheat oven to 375°F (190°C).
2. Place peach halves in a baking dish.
3. Mix maple syrup, butter, and cinnamon. Drizzle over peaches.
4. Bake for 20-25 minutes until tender.

Blackberry Oatmeal Bars

Ingredients

- 1 1/2 cups rolled oats
- 1 cup all-purpose flour
- 1/2 cup brown sugar
- 1/2 cup butter, melted
- 1/2 tsp baking soda
- 1 cup blackberries

Instructions

1. Preheat oven to 350°F (175°C) and grease an 8x8 pan.
2. Mix oats, flour, sugar, butter, and baking soda. Press half into the pan.
3. Spread blackberries over the crust and top with remaining oat mixture.
4. Bake for 25-30 minutes until golden.

Plum and Ginger Compote

Ingredients

- 4 cups plums, chopped
- 1/4 cup brown sugar
- 1 tbsp grated ginger
- 1 tbsp lemon juice

Instructions

1. In a saucepan, combine plums, sugar, ginger, and lemon juice.
2. Cook over medium heat for 15-20 minutes, stirring occasionally.
3. Serve warm or chilled.

Strawberry Shortcake

Ingredients

- 2 cups all-purpose flour
- 1/4 cup granulated sugar
- 1 tbsp baking powder
- 1/2 tsp salt
- 1/2 cup unsalted butter, cold and cubed
- 3/4 cup heavy cream
- 1 tsp vanilla extract
- 2 cups strawberries, sliced
- 2 tbsp sugar
- 1 cup whipped cream

Instructions

1. Preheat oven to 400°F (200°C). Line a baking sheet with parchment paper.
2. In a bowl, mix flour, sugar, baking powder, and salt. Cut in butter until crumbly.
3. Add cream and vanilla, stirring until dough forms.
4. Drop dough onto the baking sheet and bake for 15-18 minutes until golden.
5. Toss strawberries with sugar and let sit for 10 minutes.
6. Split shortcakes, fill with strawberries and whipped cream, and serve.

Roasted Pears with Balsamic Drizzle

Ingredients

- 4 pears, halved and cored
- 2 tbsp honey
- 1/2 tsp cinnamon
- 1/4 cup balsamic vinegar

Instructions

1. Preheat oven to 375°F (190°C).
2. Arrange pears in a baking dish, drizzle with honey, and sprinkle with cinnamon.
3. Roast for 25-30 minutes until tender.
4. Simmer balsamic vinegar over low heat until reduced by half.
5. Drizzle over pears before serving.

Apple and Cheddar Grilled Cheese

Ingredients

- 4 slices sourdough bread
- 1 apple, thinly sliced
- 1 cup sharp cheddar cheese, shredded
- 2 tbsp butter

Instructions

1. Heat a skillet over medium heat.
2. Butter one side of each bread slice.
3. Place one slice butter-side down, add cheese and apple slices, and top with another slice.
4. Cook until golden brown on both sides and cheese melts.

Raspberry Lemon Loaf

Ingredients

- 1 1/2 cups all-purpose flour
- 1 tsp baking powder
- 1/2 tsp salt
- 1/2 cup butter, softened
- 3/4 cup granulated sugar
- 2 eggs
- 1/2 cup milk
- 1 tbsp lemon zest
- 1 tbsp lemon juice
- 1 cup raspberries

Instructions

1. Preheat oven to 350°F (175°C). Grease a loaf pan.
2. In a bowl, mix flour, baking powder, and salt.
3. In another bowl, beat butter and sugar until fluffy. Add eggs, milk, zest, and juice.
4. Combine wet and dry ingredients, then fold in raspberries.
5. Pour into pan and bake for 50-55 minutes.

Ontario Peach Salsa

Ingredients

- 2 cups Ontario peaches, diced
- 1/2 cup red bell pepper, diced
- 1/4 cup red onion, minced
- 1 jalapeño, seeded and diced
- 2 tbsp lime juice
- 2 tbsp cilantro, chopped
- Salt to taste

Instructions

1. In a bowl, mix all ingredients together.
2. Let sit for 10 minutes before serving.

Wild Blueberry Pancakes

Ingredients

- 1 1/2 cups all-purpose flour
- 1 tbsp sugar
- 1 tsp baking powder
- 1/2 tsp baking soda
- 1/4 tsp salt
- 1 cup buttermilk
- 1 egg
- 2 tbsp melted butter
- 1 cup wild blueberries

Instructions

1. Preheat griddle to medium heat.
2. In a bowl, whisk flour, sugar, baking powder, baking soda, and salt.
3. In another bowl, mix buttermilk, egg, and butter. Combine wet and dry ingredients.
4. Fold in blueberries. Cook pancakes for 2-3 minutes per side.

Spiced Apple Cake

Ingredients

- 2 cups all-purpose flour
- 1 tsp baking soda
- 1/2 tsp salt
- 1 tsp cinnamon
- 1/2 tsp nutmeg
- 1/2 cup butter, softened
- 1 cup brown sugar
- 2 eggs
- 1 tsp vanilla extract
- 1/2 cup applesauce
- 2 cups apples, diced

Instructions

1. Preheat oven to 350°F (175°C). Grease a cake pan.
2. In a bowl, mix flour, baking soda, salt, cinnamon, and nutmeg.
3. In another bowl, beat butter and sugar until fluffy. Add eggs, vanilla, and applesauce.
4. Combine wet and dry ingredients, fold in apples, and pour into the pan.
5. Bake for 40-45 minutes.

Pear and Brie Crostini

Ingredients

- 1 baguette, sliced
- 2 pears, thinly sliced
- 6 oz brie cheese
- 2 tbsp honey
- 1/4 cup walnuts, chopped

Instructions

1. Preheat oven to 375°F (190°C).
2. Toast baguette slices for 5 minutes.
3. Top with brie and pear slices, then bake until cheese melts.
4. Drizzle with honey and sprinkle walnuts before serving.

Maple Apple Granola

Ingredients

- 2 cups rolled oats
- 1/2 cup chopped almonds
- 1/2 tsp cinnamon
- 1/4 cup maple syrup
- 1/4 cup coconut oil, melted
- 1/2 cup dried apples, chopped

Instructions

1. Preheat oven to 325°F (165°C).
2. In a bowl, mix oats, almonds, and cinnamon.
3. Stir in maple syrup and coconut oil. Spread on a baking sheet.
4. Bake for 20-25 minutes, stirring halfway.
5. Mix in dried apples after cooling.

Cherry Almond Scones

Ingredients

- 2 cups all-purpose flour
- 1/3 cup granulated sugar
- 1 tbsp baking powder
- 1/2 tsp salt
- 1/2 cup cold butter, cubed
- 1/2 cup chopped cherries (fresh or dried)
- 1/4 cup sliced almonds
- 1/2 cup heavy cream
- 1 egg
- 1 tsp vanilla extract

Instructions

1. Preheat oven to 375°F (190°C) and line a baking sheet with parchment paper.
2. In a bowl, mix flour, sugar, baking powder, and salt.
3. Cut in butter until the mixture resembles coarse crumbs.
4. Stir in cherries and almonds.
5. In a separate bowl, whisk cream, egg, and vanilla, then add to the dry mixture.
6. Form dough into a circle, cut into wedges, and bake for 18-20 minutes.

Cranberry Orange Bread

Ingredients

- 2 cups all-purpose flour
- 1 cup sugar
- 1 1/2 tsp baking powder
- 1/2 tsp baking soda
- 1/2 tsp salt
- 1/2 cup orange juice
- 1/2 cup butter, melted
- 2 eggs
- 1 tbsp orange zest
- 1 cup cranberries, chopped

Instructions

1. Preheat oven to 350°F (175°C). Grease a loaf pan.
2. In a bowl, mix flour, sugar, baking powder, baking soda, and salt.
3. In another bowl, whisk orange juice, butter, eggs, and zest. Combine with dry ingredients.
4. Fold in cranberries and pour into the loaf pan.
5. Bake for 50-55 minutes.

Plum Butter Spread

Ingredients

- 4 cups plums, pitted and chopped
- 1/2 cup brown sugar
- 1/2 tsp cinnamon
- 1/4 tsp nutmeg
- 1 tbsp lemon juice

Instructions

1. In a saucepan, combine all ingredients.
2. Simmer for 30-40 minutes, stirring occasionally, until thickened.
3. Blend until smooth and let cool before storing.

Strawberry Basil Sorbet

Ingredients

- 3 cups strawberries, hulled
- 1/2 cup sugar
- 1/4 cup water
- 1 tbsp lemon juice
- 4-5 basil leaves

Instructions

1. Blend all ingredients until smooth.
2. Strain if desired and freeze for 2-3 hours, stirring occasionally.

Peach and Pecan Salad

Ingredients

- 4 cups mixed greens
- 2 peaches, sliced
- 1/2 cup pecans, toasted
- 1/4 cup feta cheese
- 2 tbsp balsamic vinegar
- 2 tbsp olive oil

Instructions

1. Toss greens, peaches, pecans, and feta in a bowl.
2. Drizzle with balsamic and olive oil before serving.

Apple Cinnamon Waffles

Ingredients

- 2 cups flour
- 2 tbsp sugar
- 1 tbsp baking powder
- 1 tsp cinnamon
- 1/2 tsp salt
- 1 1/2 cups milk
- 2 eggs
- 1/4 cup melted butter
- 1 cup shredded apple

Instructions

1. Preheat waffle iron.
2. In a bowl, mix flour, sugar, baking powder, cinnamon, and salt.
3. In another bowl, whisk milk, eggs, and butter.
4. Combine wet and dry ingredients, then fold in apples.
5. Cook in a waffle iron until golden.

Blueberry Lemon Cheesecake

Ingredients

- 1 1/2 cups graham cracker crumbs
- 1/4 cup butter, melted
- 16 oz cream cheese, softened
- 3/4 cup sugar
- 2 eggs
- 1 tbsp lemon zest
- 1/4 cup lemon juice
- 1 cup blueberries

Instructions

1. Preheat oven to 325°F (160°C).
2. Mix graham crumbs and butter, then press into a springform pan.
3. Beat cream cheese and sugar until smooth. Add eggs, zest, and juice.
4. Fold in blueberries and pour over the crust.
5. Bake for 45-50 minutes and cool before chilling.

Blackberry Chia Jam

Ingredients

- 2 cups blackberries
- 2 tbsp honey
- 2 tbsp chia seeds
- 1 tbsp lemon juice

Instructions

1. Mash blackberries in a saucepan over medium heat.
2. Stir in honey and lemon juice.
3. Add chia seeds and let sit until thickened.

Raspberry Almond Tart

Ingredients

- 1 pre-made tart crust
- 1/2 cup almond flour
- 1/4 cup sugar
- 1 egg
- 1/2 tsp almond extract
- 1 cup raspberries

Instructions

1. Preheat oven to 375°F (190°C).
2. In a bowl, mix almond flour, sugar, egg, and almond extract.
3. Spread over crust and top with raspberries.
4. Bake for 30 minutes.

Apple Fritter Donuts

Ingredients

- 2 cups flour
- 1/4 cup sugar
- 2 tsp baking powder
- 1/2 tsp cinnamon
- 1/2 tsp salt
- 3/4 cup milk
- 1 egg
- 1 cup chopped apples
- Oil for frying

Instructions

1. Heat oil to 350°F (175°C).
2. In a bowl, mix flour, sugar, baking powder, cinnamon, and salt.
3. Stir in milk, egg, and apples.
4. Drop spoonfuls into hot oil and fry until golden.

Plum and Honey Yogurt Parfait

Ingredients

- 2 ripe plums, diced
- 2 cups Greek yogurt
- 2 tbsp honey
- 1/2 cup granola
- 1/4 tsp cinnamon

Instructions

1. Layer yogurt, plums, honey, and granola in a glass.
2. Repeat layers and sprinkle cinnamon on top.
3. Serve immediately.

Ontario Orchard Fruit Salad

Ingredients

- 1 apple, diced
- 1 pear, diced
- 1 peach, sliced
- 1/2 cup grapes
- 1/4 cup blueberries
- 1 tbsp honey
- 1 tbsp lemon juice

Instructions

1. Toss all fruit in a bowl.
2. Drizzle with honey and lemon juice.
3. Serve chilled.

Baked Peaches with Vanilla Ice Cream

Ingredients

- 4 peaches, halved and pitted
- 2 tbsp honey
- 1 tsp cinnamon
- 1 tbsp butter
- Vanilla ice cream

Instructions

1. Preheat oven to 375°F (190°C).
2. Place peaches in a baking dish, drizzle with honey, and sprinkle with cinnamon.
3. Top each with butter and bake for 20 minutes.
4. Serve warm with vanilla ice cream.

Maple Cranberry Sauce

Ingredients

- 2 cups cranberries
- 1/2 cup maple syrup
- 1/2 cup orange juice
- 1/2 tsp cinnamon

Instructions

1. In a saucepan, combine cranberries, maple syrup, and orange juice.
2. Simmer until cranberries burst, about 10 minutes.
3. Stir in cinnamon and let cool.

Apple Cider Doughnuts

Ingredients

- 2 cups flour
- 1/2 cup sugar
- 1 1/2 tsp baking powder
- 1/2 tsp baking soda
- 1 tsp cinnamon
- 1/4 tsp nutmeg
- 1/2 cup apple cider
- 1/2 cup buttermilk
- 1 egg
- 3 tbsp melted butter

Instructions

1. Preheat oven to 350°F (175°C). Grease a doughnut pan.
2. Mix flour, sugar, baking powder, baking soda, cinnamon, and nutmeg.
3. In another bowl, whisk apple cider, buttermilk, egg, and butter. Combine with dry ingredients.
4. Pipe batter into the pan and bake for 12-15 minutes.

Peach and Raspberry Galette

Ingredients

- 1 pie crust
- 2 peaches, sliced
- 1 cup raspberries
- 2 tbsp sugar
- 1 tbsp cornstarch
- 1 tsp lemon juice
- 1 egg (for egg wash)

Instructions

1. Preheat oven to 375°F (190°C).
2. Toss peaches, raspberries, sugar, cornstarch, and lemon juice in a bowl.
3. Roll out pie crust and place filling in the center. Fold edges over.
4. Brush crust with egg wash and bake for 35-40 minutes.

Blueberry Lavender Syrup

Ingredients

- 1 cup blueberries
- 1/2 cup sugar
- 1/2 cup water
- 1 tsp dried lavender

Instructions

1. Simmer all ingredients in a saucepan for 10 minutes.
2. Strain and let cool before using.

Pear and Maple Smoothie

Ingredients

- 1 ripe pear, chopped
- 1 cup almond milk
- 1 tbsp maple syrup
- 1/4 tsp cinnamon
- 1/2 cup ice

Instructions

1. Blend all ingredients until smooth.
2. Serve chilled.

Blackberry Honey Butter

Ingredients

- 1/2 cup butter, softened
- 1/4 cup blackberries, mashed
- 1 tbsp honey

Instructions

1. Whip butter, blackberries, and honey together.
2. Store in the fridge until ready to use.

Spiced Plum Cake

Ingredients

- 1 1/2 cups flour
- 1/2 cup sugar
- 1 tsp cinnamon
- 1/2 tsp nutmeg
- 1/2 tsp baking powder
- 1/2 tsp baking soda
- 1/2 cup butter, melted
- 2 eggs
- 1/2 cup buttermilk
- 2 cups plums, sliced

Instructions

1. Preheat oven to 350°F (175°C). Grease a cake pan.
2. Mix dry ingredients in one bowl.
3. In another bowl, whisk butter, eggs, and buttermilk. Combine with dry ingredients.
4. Fold in plums and pour into the pan.
5. Bake for 40-45 minutes.

Roasted Apple and Squash Soup

Ingredients

- 1 butternut squash, peeled and cubed
- 2 apples, cored and chopped
- 1 onion, chopped
- 3 cups vegetable broth
- 1/2 cup coconut milk or heavy cream
- 1 tsp cinnamon
- 1/2 tsp nutmeg
- 2 tbsp olive oil
- Salt and pepper to taste

Instructions

1. Preheat oven to 400°F (200°C). Toss squash, apples, and onion with olive oil, then roast for 30 minutes.
2. Transfer to a pot, add broth, and bring to a boil. Simmer for 10 minutes.
3. Blend until smooth, stir in coconut milk, and season with cinnamon, nutmeg, salt, and pepper.
4. Serve warm.

Strawberry Rhubarb Compote

Ingredients

- 2 cups strawberries, hulled and chopped
- 2 cups rhubarb, chopped
- 1/2 cup sugar
- 1 tbsp lemon juice
- 1 tsp vanilla extract

Instructions

1. In a saucepan, combine all ingredients.
2. Simmer over medium heat for 15-20 minutes until fruit softens.
3. Mash slightly and let cool before serving.

Cranberry and Brie Puff Pastry Bites

Ingredients

- 1 sheet puff pastry, thawed
- 4 oz brie cheese, cut into cubes
- 1/2 cup cranberry sauce
- 1 egg (for egg wash)

Instructions

1. Preheat oven to 375°F (190°C) and line a baking sheet with parchment paper.
2. Cut puff pastry into small squares and place on the sheet.
3. Add a cube of brie and a spoonful of cranberry sauce to each square.
4. Fold edges slightly, brush with egg wash, and bake for 15-18 minutes.

Apple Walnut Bread

Ingredients

- 2 cups all-purpose flour
- 1 tsp baking soda
- 1/2 tsp salt
- 1 tsp cinnamon
- 1/2 cup butter, melted
- 1 cup sugar
- 2 eggs
- 1 tsp vanilla extract
- 1/2 cup milk
- 1 1/2 cups apples, diced
- 1/2 cup walnuts, chopped

Instructions

1. Preheat oven to 350°F (175°C). Grease a loaf pan.
2. Mix flour, baking soda, salt, and cinnamon in a bowl.
3. In another bowl, whisk butter, sugar, eggs, vanilla, and milk.
4. Combine with dry ingredients, fold in apples and walnuts.
5. Pour into pan and bake for 50-55 minutes.

Maple Baked Apples with Oat Topping

Ingredients

- 4 apples, cored
- 1/4 cup rolled oats
- 2 tbsp maple syrup
- 1/4 tsp cinnamon
- 1 tbsp butter, melted

Instructions

1. Preheat oven to 375°F (190°C).
2. Mix oats, maple syrup, cinnamon, and butter in a bowl.
3. Fill apples with oat mixture and place in a baking dish.
4. Bake for 25-30 minutes until tender.

Ontario Orchard Harvest Jam

Ingredients

- 2 cups apples, peeled and chopped
- 1 cup pears, chopped
- 1 cup peaches, chopped
- 1/2 cup cranberries
- 2 cups sugar
- 1 tbsp lemon juice
- 1 tsp cinnamon

Instructions

1. In a pot, combine all ingredients and bring to a boil.
2. Simmer for 30-40 minutes until thickened.
3. Blend slightly if desired, then pour into sterilized jars.

www.ingramcontent.com/pod-product-compliance
Lightning Source LLC
LaVergne TN
LVHW081342060526
838201LV00055B/2811